preteen Bible study series

God in My Life

Group

Loveland, Colorado

Group's R.E.A.L. Guarantee to you:

This Group resource incorporates our R.E.A.L. approach to ministry—one that encourages long-term retention and life transformation. It's ministry that's:

Relational

Because learner-to-learner interaction enhances learning and builds Christian friendships.

Experiential

Because what learners experience through discussion and action sticks with them up to 9 times longer than what they simply hear or read.

Applicable

Because the aim of Christian education is to equip learners to be both hearers and doers of God's Word.

Learner-based

Because learners understand and retain more when the learning process takes into consideration how they learn best.

preteen Bible study series

God in My Life

Copyright © 2003 Group Publishing, Inc.

Visit our Web site: **www.grouppublishing.com**

Credits
Authors: Dr. Dick Hardel, Larry Keefauver, Walter H. Mees Jr.
Editor: Jim Hawley
Creative Development Editor: Karl Leuthauser
Chief Creative Officer: Joani Schultz
Copy Editor: Lyndsay E. Gerwing
Art Director: Kari K. Monson
Cover Art Director/Designer: Jeff A. Storm
Cover Photographer: Daniel Treat
Print Production Artist: Joyce Douglas
Illustrator: Shawn Banner
Production Manager: DeAnne Lear

ISBN 0-7644-2471-8
10 9 8 7 6 5 4 3 2 1   12 11 10 09 08 07 06 05 04 03

Printed in the United States of America.

Contents

Introduction:
God in My Life

As preteens mature, they are beginning to challenge the assumptions of previously learned things. Many preteens have grown up hearing Bible stories and now are faced with owning the truths found in those stories.

As a foundation to their faith, exploring the fact of God in three persons, commonly called the Trinity, is an important place to begin. The series of studies in *God in My Life* will help preteens explore Bible truths about God, Jesus, and the Holy Spirit.

The first study will explore God as a loving father and help preteens develop a close relationship with their "Abba" Father, even if they don't have a positive relationship with their earthly fathers. Next preteens will discover how Jesus is both human and divine and how this understanding will strengthen their faith. The third study explores the role of the Holy Spirit as teacher and guide, and the last study encourages personal commitment to Jesus as preteens discover how Jesus can be their very best friend.

> Many preteens have grown up hearing Bible stories and now are faced with owning the truths found in those stories.

About Faith 4 Life: Preteen Bible Study Series

The Faith 4 Life: Preteen Bible Study Series helps preteens take a Bible-based approach to faith and life issues. Each book in the series contains these important elements:

- **Life application of Bible truth**—Faith 4 Life studies help preteens understand what the Bible says, and then apply that truth to their lives.

- **A relevant topic**—Each Faith 4 Life book focuses on one main topic, with four studies to give your students a thorough understanding of how the Bible relates to that topic.

- **One point**—Each study makes one point, centering on that one theme to make sure students really understand the important truth it conveys. This point is stated upfront and throughout the study.

- **Simplicity**—The studies are easy to use. Each contains a "Before the Study" box that outlines any advance preparation required. Each study also contains a "Study at a Glance" chart so you can quickly and easily see what supplies you'll need and what each study will involve.

- **Action and interaction**—Each study relies on experiential learning to help students learn what God's Word has to say. Preteens discuss and debrief their experiences in large groups, small groups, and individual reflection.

- **Reproducible handouts**—Faith 4 Life books include reproducible handouts for students. No need for student books!

- **Flexible options**—Faith 4 Life preteen studies have two opening and two closing activities. You can choose the options that work best for your students, time frame, or supply needs.

- **Follow-up ideas**—At the end of each book, you'll find a section called "Changed 4 Life." This provides ideas for following up with your students to make sure the Bible truths stick with them.

Use Faith 4 Life studies to show your preteens how the Bible is relevant to their lives. Help them see that God can invade every area of their lives and change them in ways they can only imagine. Encourage your students to go deeper into faith—faith that will sustain them for life! Faith 4 Life, forever!

God as Father

The Point: ➤ God wants us to have a close relationship with him.

hen God the Son walked the earth and was known as Jesus, he spoke often of his wonderful relationship with God. He actually called God "Abba," which means "daddy," from the cross. Preteens' relationships with their parents are often strained. And because so many families are broken or dysfunctional, many kids don't know the wonderful love a father can have for his children. By looking at Jesus' relationship with his Father, preteens can see a model of fatherly love that far exceeds any earthly love.

Scripture Source

Psalm 68:4-5

David reminds us to praise God for taking care of all who need him. God particularly looks after widows and orphans, acting as husband to those with no husbands and father to those with no fathers.

In this day of so many broken marriages, God's promise here is very important and should be shared with all who are affected by divorce and other tragedies.

Matthew 6:9-13

Jesus teaches the disciples how to pray. The Lord's Prayer, as these verses are commonly called, is a model prayer that Jesus gives to help us focus on the most important elements of a prayerful life.

Matthew 7:9-11

Jesus describes God's willingness to give good gifts to his children. Jesus tells us that if most human, sinful fathers take care of their children, we can trust God even more to love and take care of us.

Luke 15:11-32

Jesus tells the story of the lost son. The younger son shows great disrespect to his father by demanding his inheritance. After the father gives him the share, the son loses it all in wild living. The son comes to his senses and returns to the father, who throws a party for his once lost son. The older brother is angry, but the father explains that while the older son has always been faithful, he is thankful that his younger son has returned.

Hebrews 12:9-11

The writer describes how God the Father disciplines his children as an earthly father does. The pain from discipline leads to our sharing in God's holiness and peace.

James 1:16-18

James says that every good gift is from God. This passage includes both a warning and a promise. The warning is against falling into deception and thinking we've earned the good things we have or that they're from someone other than God. The promise is that God has not only given us all good things, but he has also created each of us to play a special role in the universe.

The Study at a Glance

Section	Minutes	What Students Will Do	Supplies
Warm-Up Option 1	up to 10	**Names for God**—List different names for God.	Bibles, newsprint, tape, marker
Warm-Up Option 2	up to 10	**Why Dad's All Right**—Tell why they like their fathers or friends' fathers.	
Bible Connection	up to 20	**Care and Comfort**—Experience being cared for and guided and explore the father's response to his lost son in Luke 15.	Bibles, paper cups, books, newsprint, tape, markers, blindfolds
	up to 15	**The Best Father of All**—Discover how God is the ultimate Father.	Bibles, markers or crayons, newsprint, tape
Life Application	up to 15	**"Abba" Covenant**—Commit to relate to God as Father.	"*Abba* Means Father" handouts (p. 15), pens
Wrap-Up Option 1	up to 10	**Our Father**—Write personal versions of the Lord's Prayer.	Bibles, paper, pens
Wrap-Up Option 2	up to 5	**Song to the Father**—Sing a familiar song about God's love.	Songbooks

Before the Study

Set out Bibles, books, blindfolds for every two preteens, paper, pens, newsprint, markers, tape, paper cups, and songbooks. Make enough photocopies of the "*Abba* Means Father" handout (p. 15) for each preteen to have one. Also prepare instruction sheets for the "Care and Comfort" activity (pp. 10-11).

The Study

Some of your kids may not have positive relationships with their fathers. Some may not live with their dads. If you know of kids in these situations, be sensitive to their feelings. They may not be able to think of a "father" figure as a positive thing. This study is designed to help kids feel good talking about fathers, even if they don't have good experiences with their own fathers.

Warm-Up Option 1

Names for God *(up to 10 minutes)*

Tape a sheet of newsprint to the wall. As kids arrive, take note of the person who arrived first. Have that person be the "scribe" for this opening activity.

Say: To begin today's study, I'd like to have you brainstorm names for God. You have three minutes to come up with as many names as you can. If you'd like to, you may look at a Bible. See if you can fill the newsprint with names. I'll start by suggesting the name *Abba*. I'll explain what *Abba* means a bit later. Ready? Begin.

Have the scribe list names as kids come up with them. After three minutes, call time. Thank the scribe for helping. **Ask:**

- **How did you feel as you tried to come up with names for God?**
- **How is that like the way people feel when they try to understand God?**
- **Why are there so many different names for God?**

Say: People see God in many different ways. In the Bible we can find many names for God, each with a different meaning. But one of the most meaningful names for God is *Abba*. This name is meaningful because it means "father" or "daddy." Today's lesson will help us see the Bible's picture of God as our heavenly Father. We'll discover why ➤God wants us to have a close relationship with him.

◄ *The Point*

Warm-Up Option 2

Why Dad's All Right *(up to 10 minutes)*

Have kids pair up, and have each partner tell the other a brief story about a time his or her dad or a friend's dad did something particularly special with or for him or her. After three minutes, have one or two pairs briefly act out or describe one of the times they discussed.

Then **ask:**
- **What do these stories say about dads?**
- **When you think of the perfect father, what comes to mind?**

Say: Today our study will help us focus on God the Father and the

extra-special relationship he has with his Son, Jesus. And we'll discover how ➤God wants us to have a close relationship with him.

Bible Connection

Care and Comfort *(up to 20 minutes)*

Before the study, copy each of the following instructions onto a separate sheet of newsprint. Hide the four sheets of newsprint so that kids can't see what's written on them. You'll be taping them to the wall during the activity.

First Instruction: Don't assist your partner in any way. Let him or her fail.

Second Instruction: Call out encouragement to your partner, but don't help him or her.

Third Instruction: Help guide your partner's hand to draw the elephant.

Fourth Instruction: When the activity's over, comfort your partner and congratulate him or her for doing good work.

Place a supply of paper cups, books, newsprint, and markers around the room.

Have kids form pairs and each look around the room to observe where the supplies are. Then have one partner in each pair put on a blindfold.

Say: Each person wearing a blindfold will be asked to complete a few tasks that I'll describe. Do your best to complete each task as I describe it.

During the activity, I'll also give instructions to the sighted partners by calling out, "New instructions," and taping signs onto the wall explaining what they're to do. To begin, the partners without blindfolds may only ensure that their partners don't injure themselves while following my directions.

When a blindfolded partner thinks he or she has completed the action I've requested, call me over and I'll check your work.

Instruct the blindfolded partners to each find ten paper cups and stack them in a pyramid shape on the floor. Tell kids that the pyramid may have only four cups on the bottom level.

As blindfolded kids begin this task, call out, "New instructions," and tape up the instruction sign labeled "First Instruction." Tell kids without blindfolds not to read the instructions aloud.

When the cup pyramids are complete, or after a couple of minutes of unsuccessful attempts, call out this next instruction. **Say: Now you must each find a book and balance it on your head.**

As blindfolded kids begin to complete this task, call out, "New instructions," and tape up the instruction sign labeled "Second Instruction."

When kids have each attempted to balance a book, or after a couple of minutes of unsuccessful attempts, **say: Now find a sheet of newsprint and a marker, and draw a picture of an elephant on it.**

Call out, "New instructions," and tape up the instruction sign labeled "Third Instruction."

While the sighted partners are helping their partners draw the pictures of the elephants, call out, "New instructions," one more time, and tape up the instruction sign labeled "Fourth Instruction."

After another minute or so, have the blindfolded kids take off their blindfolds. Have them look around at the pyramids and the elephant drawings. Allow a minute or so for the sighted partners to comfort and congratulate their partners.

Form a circle, and direct these questions to the kids who were blindfolded. **Ask:**

• **How did you feel during the first part of this activity?**

• **How did you feel as you received encouragement from your partner during the second activity?**

• **How did you feel as you received guidance during the third activity?**

• **How did you feel as you were comforted and congratulated for your efforts after the activities were completed?**

Have kids re-form their pairs, and give each pair a Bible. Have partners take turns reading aloud about five verses each from Luke 15:11-32. When partners have finished reading the story, have them discuss the following question. **Ask:**

• **How are the ways your partner cared for you or watched over you like the way the father cared for his children in this story?**

Show everyone the newsprint instructions you used during the activity. **Say: Each instruction I gave to the sighted partners illustrates one aspect of a father's love for his children—allowing them to fail, encouraging them, guiding them, and comforting them. Even the instruction I gave to keep the blindfolded partner from getting hurt illustrates one way a good father cares for his children.**

Direct these questions to the sighted partners. **Ask:**

• **How did you feel when you had to allow your partner to fail?**

• **How do you think the father felt allowing his son to leave in the story?**

• **How did you feel when you were able to help your partner? Explain.**

• **How do you think God feels when he is able to help his children?**

Say: Jesus told this story to show us the kind of love the Father has for all

FYI

Whenever groups discuss a list of questions, write the questions on newsprint, and tape the newsprint to the wall so that groups can discuss the questions at their own pace.

his children. When the son returned, the father threw a huge party. He was excited that his lost son had returned. Just as the son discovered in this story, **➤God wants to have a close relationship with you and me.** Let's look at some more ways we can know this.

The Point ➤ **➤**

The Best Father of All *(up to 15 minutes)*

Say: When we see God as our Father, we see the perfect example of a father. Even if your relationship hasn't been good with your father, you can find a tremendous relationship with God as Father. Let's explore this further.

Have kids form groups of no more than four. A group can be two people. Give each group a Bible, markers or crayons, and a sheet of newsprint. Assign each group one of the following Bible passages: Psalm 68:4-5; Matthew 7:9-11; Hebrews 12:9-11; and James 1:16-18.

Say: The Bible makes some pretty amazing promises about how God treats us, his human children. Have the youngest member of your group read your group's verses aloud. Then talk in your group about how the passage depicts God as Father, and work together to draw a poster illustrating the meaning of the passage.

When five minutes are up, ask each group to show its poster and explain how it illustrates the passage the group read. Tape the posters to the wall. **Ask:**

• **What do these posters, and the Scriptures, tell us about God as Father?**

• **What makes God a good Father?**

Say: God is a Father who wants a close relationship with each of his children. Let's see how we can develop a closer relationship with God.

Life Application

"Abba" Covenant *(up to 15 minutes)*

Give each preteen an *"Abba* Means Father" handout (p. 15) and a pen. Have kids complete the handouts, and allow preteens to share some of their responses with the larger group. Then have kids form pairs. **Say:** In your pairs, I want you to create brief skits in which you show something you've learned about God being "Abba" Father. One of you will play the part of the Father, and the other will play the role of yourself. You may use the responses on your "*Abba* Means Father" handout if you'd like. After you've created one skit, switch roles and create another one.

Give kids a few minutes to prepare their skits. Then have pairs perform their skits.

Ask:

• **How did your skits help you see the way to have a closer relationship with God?**

• **What things do you need to do to improve your relationship with God?**

Say: God is our perfect Father. We can always count on him to do everything. A covenant is a promise between two people. Since we know that God will always live up to his part of the covenant, we are left with the challenge of loving and obeying God. I'd like you to silently reread your "Abba" Covenant as a prayer of commitment to God.

Have preteens silently reread their "Abba" Covenants before moving to the closing activity.

Wrap-Up Option 1

Our Father *(up to 10 minutes)*

Have a volunteer read aloud Matthew 6:9-13. **Say: This prayer depicts God as our Father and describes some of the ways he cares for his children. Find a partner, and take three minutes to write your own version of this prayer, emphasizing the ways God takes care of you as your Father. We'll read these aloud as our closing prayer.**

Give pairs Bibles, paper, and pens. After three minutes or so, have pairs read aloud their prayers to the larger group. Close in prayer, asking God to be their loving Father.

Wrap-Up Option 2

Song to the Father *(up to 5 minutes)*

Form a circle, and sing a familiar song about God's role as Father. For example, you might choose "This Is My Father's World" or "Father, I Adore You." If necessary, have songbooks available for kids to follow along with the words. Let the song be sung as a closing prayer to God, thanking him for being a Father to his children.

Extra-Time Tips

Use these extra ideas to add some creative fun to your studies. They are low-prep or no-prep ideas that work in no time!

Making Tomorrow Father's Day—Have kids form groups of no more than three and tell about Father's Day gifts their fathers really liked. Have kids brainstorm creative ways to thank their fathers for "just being dad." Have groups report their ideas to the rest of the groups. Have kids vote on the "best" idea and commit to carry out the winning idea for their dads tomorrow. Have kids who don't have fathers at home each choose an adult they respect to show their appreciation to.

A Letter to My Father—Distribute a pen, two sheets of paper, and two envelopes to each person. Ask kids to write brief letters of thanks to God for being their ultimate Father. Then have kids who feel comfortable doing so write similar letters to their earthly fathers. Encourage kids to keep their letters to God as reminders of God's love for them. Also, have kids deliver or mail their letters to their dads.

Abba Means Father

Complete the following sentences, then read and complete the covenant at the bottom of the page.

• Knowing that God is my father makes me feel _____ because

• Qualities that make God a great "dad" include

• One thing I can learn from my heavenly Father that may help my relationship with my earthly father is

• Ways I can develop my relationship with my heavenly Father include

· ·

"Abba" COVENANT

The following agreement was reached this _____ day of _____, in the year _____,

between _____ and God.

I will seek to obey God as a loving child obeys his or her loving father. I will stay near God through prayer and

Bible reading so he can give me the peace he promises. I will seek God's will and trust him for answers to life's

problems. And I will honor my earthly parents because my heavenly Father wants me to.

Signed: _____

Jesus: God and Human

The Point: ➤ Jesus is both human and divine.

f asked the question "Who is Jesus?" many preteens wouldn't know how to respond. They might answer that Jesus was a good person…and nothing else. Or they might decide Jesus couldn't have been both human and divine.

Today's non-Christian beliefs portray Jesus in many different ways—ways that don't always match the Bible's portrayal of Jesus. By exploring the Bible's picture of Jesus as truly God and truly human, preteens can learn to confidently answer the question "Who is Jesus?"

Scripture Source

Luke 24:36-48

This passage describes Jesus' appearance to the disciples and others following his resurrection. Luke draws attention to Jesus' hands and feet and his hunger to establish that he is indeed a human being, not a ghost or spirit.

John 1:1-18

As John describes the "Word" that was with God from the beginning of time, he is describing Jesus. This passage is significant because it helps us see a connection between our lives and our faith in Jesus Christ. John wants us to understand that the Word became flesh—that God became a human being.

Hebrews 4:14-15

This passage talks about how Jesus is our high priest. The high priest sacrificed animals to receive God's forgiveness for all of his people. In the same way, Jesus sacrificed himself and went before God to receive forgiveness for all the people who believe in Jesus.

The Study at a Glance

Section	Minutes	What Students Will Do	Supplies
Warm-Up Option 1	up to 5	**Line Up**—Line up on a continuum based on their responses to statements about Jesus.	Masking tape
Warm-Up Option 2	up to 10	**Picture This**—List words describing who Jesus is.	Newsprint, markers, tape
Bible Connection	up to 20	**Acting or Becoming?**—Observe and act like preschoolers and then compare the experience to Luke 24:36-48.	Bible, index cards, pens, preschool toys
	up to 15	**Making the Word Come Alive**—Describe hidden objects and explore John 1:1-18.	Bibles, blindfolds, box of miscellaneous items
Life Application	up to 15	**I Still Have Questions**—Write and share responses to statements about Jesus.	"Jesus Questions" handouts (p. 24), pens
Wrap-Up Option 1	up to 5	**High Priest**—Read Hebrews 4:14-15 and thank God for Jesus' sacrifice.	Bible
Wrap-Up Option 2	up to 10	**Just Like Me**—Mold clay to represent how they feel about Jesus and pray for each other.	Blindfolds, modeling clay

Before the Study

Set out Bibles, a blindfold for each preteen, masking tape, pens, an assortment of common objects (see p. 21), modeling clay, newsprint, markers, tape, index cards, and preschool toys. Also make enough photocopies of the "Jesus Questions" handout (p. 24) for each preteen to have one.

The Study

Warm-Up Option 1

Line Up (up to 5 minutes)

Use masking tape to draw a line down the middle of the floor. **Say: After I read a statement, stand along the line according to how you feel about the statement. This end** (point to one end of the line) **means you agree completely, and the other end** (point to the other end of the line) **means you disagree completely.**

Read aloud each of the following statements. Allow time for kids to each find a spot to stand along the continuum.

- **Most of my friends think Jesus was a great man.**
- **Jesus is God.**

- Jesus was a good teacher.
- Jesus walked the earth as a human.
- Jesus never really died.
- Jesus rose from the dead.
- Jesus is both human and divine.
- If someone asked me who Jesus is, I could confidently explain who he is.
- I'd like to know more about who Jesus is.

Have kids sit down. Then **ask:**

- **What did you notice about the way people responded to these statements?**
- **How did you feel as you decided how to respond?**
- **How is that like the way some people feel when they think about who Jesus is?**

Say: These statements are ones that different people could make about Jesus. Today we're going to explore some things the Bible tells us about Jesus. One of the amazing things is ►Jesus is both human and divine. Let's see how knowing this can help you grow closer to God.

◄ *The Point*

Warm-Up Option 2

Picture This *(up to 10 minutes)*

Draw two large picture frames on newsprint, and tape them to opposite walls. Have kids form two teams, and give each team one marker. Have team members line up in the center of the room, each team facing a different newsprint frame.

Say: When I say "go," one person from each team must run up to his or her newsprint to write a one- or two-word response to the question "Who is Jesus?" The response can be something you believe about Jesus or something someone else believes. Then team members must run back to their teams and hand the marker to the next person in line. This person must then run up and follow the same instructions.

We'll continue, with one person from each team writing at a time, until I say stop. The object is to come up with a word-picture of Jesus.

Say "go," and allow three to five minutes for teams to compete. Then call time, and have teams compare their "pictures" of Jesus.

Ask:

- **How did you feel as you tried to think of a description of Jesus?**

• **How is that like the way some people feel when they try to understand who Jesus is?**

Say: Each of us probably has a different picture of who Jesus is. But the best place to get an accurate picture of Jesus is the Bible. Today we're going to explore some things the Bible tells us about Jesus. One of the amazing

The Point ➤

things is ➤Jesus is both human and divine. Let's see how knowing this can help you grow closer to God.

Bible Connection

Acting or Becoming? *(up to 20 minutes)*

Arrange ahead of time with a preschool or kindergarten teacher to have your kids visit his or her class briefly during this study.

FYI

If a class isn't available to visit, skip the first part of this activity, and ask the questions that follow based on what preteens have observed in the past about preschoolers.

Give each preteen an index card and a pen. **Say:** We're going to visit a preschool class in progress. Try not to distract the kids while you observe them. As you watch the little ones, make notes about what you see them do. List actions, emotions, and any other observations you might have.

Take the preteens to the class or classes you prearranged to visit. After three to five minutes, have your students return to your classroom. Have kids tell what they observed about the preschoolers. Then **ask:**

• **What's difficult about observing the children from a distance?**

• **Did you fully appreciate how the children felt and what they thought just by observing them? Explain.**

Pull out the preschool toys, and give them to the class members. Ask students to become like little children and play for a few minutes with the toys. Encourage class members to sit on the floor or walk on their knees to help them get the proper perspective. Also, have kids talk as if they were young children, using only simple words and sentences.

After a few minutes, collect the toys and **ask:**

• **How did you feel playing with preschool toys?**

• **What did you discover about children by becoming like a little child?**

• **How is the information you learned while "being" little children different from what you learned while observing little children?**

Say: When Jesus was raised from the dead, he appeared to his disciples, who couldn't believe it was really Jesus.

Have a volunteer read Luke 24:36-48 aloud.

Ask:

• **Why do you think the disciples had a hard time believing Jesus was alive?**

• **How do these verses show Jesus' humanity?**

• **How do these verses show Jesus' divinity?**

Say: **In our activity, you couldn't actually become children; you could only observe them or act like them. But when Jesus appeared to his disciples, he showed them ➤ he is both human and divine. The disciples were able to touch Jesus to see he was human, and him standing in front of them after being killed on a cross showed Jesus' divinity. Now let's explore more of what it means for God to become human.**

◀ *The Point*

Making the Word Come Alive *(up to 15 minutes)*

Have kids sit in a circle and each put on a blindfold. **Say:** **I'm going to give some of you items to describe to the rest of the class. When I give the item to you, take a few seconds to describe the object without naming it or saying what it's used for. You may not know what it is, and that's all right.**

Give someone in the circle an item from a box of miscellaneous items. Your box might include common things (such as paper clips, key rings, pencils, and bottle caps) or other, more obscure items (such as parts from computers, stereos, or other mechanical items).

Allow the volunteer up to twenty seconds to describe his or her item. Then **say:** **Before I pass this item around, make a mental snapshot of what you think it looks and feels like.**

Pause, then have the volunteer pass the item around. Repeat this activity as time permits so that other kids can attempt to describe items.

After volunteers have described their items and passed them around, have kids remove their blindfolds.

Ask:

• **What was it like as you tried to describe the item you were holding?**

• **How did your mental picture of each item change when you got to hold the item?**

Ask several volunteers to take turns reading verses aloud from John 1:1-18.

Ask:

• **How is what God did by becoming flesh like what you did when you** held the items from our last activity in your hands?

Have kids place the items from this activity in the center of the circle. Have kids in turn choose one item from the pile and explain how it represents something about Jesus as human or divine. For example, someone who picks up a pencil might say, "If Jesus walked the earth today, he could actually use this pencil," or "Jesus has the power to create the tree that this pencil was made from, but he chose to walk among the trees with us." Encourage kids to be creative in their descriptions of Jesus.

Say: **As we explore what the Bible says about Jesus, we may discover more questions than answers. Don't be afraid to ask your questions and dig deeper. The more we learn about Jesus, the more we'll want to know.**

Life Application

I Still Have Questions *(up to 15 minutes)*

Give each preteen a "Jesus Questions" handout (p. 24) and a pen. **Say:** **On your question mark, write your name, then write your responses to the three sentences on the first set of lines after the sentences.**

Have kids form groups of up to three and exchange handouts within their groups. **Say:** **One way we can learn more about Jesus is to hear what others have learned. On your group members' handouts, write your own responses to the three sentences. Each of you should write on each group member's handout.**

Give kids a few minutes to write responses on their group members' papers. Then have kids retrieve their papers and read the responses from other group members. **Ask:**

• **What new things did you learn about Jesus from your group members?**

• **How can the words and encouragement from other Christians help you know Jesus more?**

The Point ➤   **Say:** **We've looked at just a few ways ➤Jesus is both human and divine. Through reading the Bible, learning from other Christians, and prayer, we can grow closer to Jesus.**

Wrap-Up Option 1

High Priest *(up to 5 minutes)*

Read aloud Hebrews 4:14-15. **Say:** **This passage talks about how Jesus is our high priest. The high priest sacrificed animals to receive God's forgiveness** for all of his people. In the same way, Jesus sacrificed himself and went before God to receive forgiveness for all the people who believe in Jesus. And because Jesus became fully human, he understands all the temptations we face.

Have kids take a few minutes to silently reflect on Jesus' sacrifice for them, before closing in prayer.

Wrap-Up Option 2

Just Like Me (up to 10 minutes)

Have preteens form groups of no more than six, sit in circles in their groups, and put on their blindfolds. **Say:** I'm going to pass a piece of modeling clay around the circle to my right. I'll first shape it to represent how I feel about Jesus before passing it around. When you receive the clay, use your fingers to examine the shape, then pray silently for the person who handed you the clay. Then reshape the clay to represent how you feel about Jesus, and pass it to the next person. We'll continue this until each person has prayed for the person on the left and reshaped the clay.

When the clay returns to you, say "amen" and dismiss the class.

FYI

Play quiet music while the clay is passed around the circle.

Extra-Time Tips

Use these extra ideas to add some creative fun to your studies. They are low-prep or no-prep ideas that work in no time!

Other Views—Invite your pastor to talk about religious groups that have a different viewpoint about Jesus' humanity or divinity. Or simply have kids discuss the following questions:

• **If you have faith in God, does it really matter what you believe about Jesus? Explain.**

• **What's wrong with groups that believe Jesus was a great teacher but not God?**

• **Why is it important that Jesus was both God and human?**

Dramatic Picture—Have kids create and perform a short skit or drama based on Luke 24:36-48 and discuss it afterward.

Jesus Questions

- If Jesus is truly God and truly human, that means I...

- A question that I still have about Jesus is...

- One thing I can do to get to know Jesus better is...

The Holy Spirit: Our Teacher and Guide

The Point: ➤ The Holy Spirit teaches and guides us.

It's not easy for preteens to sift through the many decisions they face in search of God's will. Yet they can know God has provided a way for us to be taught spiritual truth and to follow God's direction. The Holy Spirit reveals and instructs us daily in God's will for our lives. As we live by the Spirit, Christian qualities will be evident in our lives. Use this study to help preteens experience life in the Spirit.

Scripture Source

John 14:26; 16:6-16

Jesus tells the disciples some of what the Holy Spirit will do but further promises them that they will learn all his teaching when the Holy Spirit is sent upon them. The Holy Spirit will teach them what belongs to Jesus and God, clearly showing the interconnection of the Godhead.

Romans 8:9-16

Paul writes that as God's children we're led by the Spirit, not the sinful nature. The Holy Spirit controls our attitudes and actions that reflect God's nature and purpose within us.

Galatians 5:22-23a

Paul writes about the fruit of the Spirit—qualities of love, joy, peace, patience, kindness, goodness, faithfulness, gentleness, and self-control—that are evidences of people living by the Spirit.

Section	Minutes	What Students Will Do	Supplies
Warm-Up Option 1	up to 10	**How Much Guidance Do You Need?**—Put puzzles together with or without assistance.	3 children's puzzles
Warm-Up Option 2	up to 10	**Looking for Guidance**—Compete in a relay race and compare the Holy Spirit with balloons.	Balloons
Bible Connection	up to 20	**Finding Our Way in the Dark**—Find their way blindfolded through an obstacle course, before exploring John 14.	Bibles, blindfolds, chairs, "Let the Spirit Speak" handouts (p. 32), pens
	up to 15	**A Personal Holy Spirit**—Write Romans 8:9-16 in their own words.	Bibles, paper, pens
Life Application	up to 10	**Fruit in My Life**—Complete "The Spirit's Fruit" handouts.	Bibles, "The Spirit's Fruit" handouts (p. 33), pencils
Wrap-Up Option 1	up to 5	**Anointing Power**—Pray for guidance from the Holy Spirit.	
Wrap-Up Option 2	up to 5	**A Fruitful Prayer**—Ask God to grow the fruit of the Spirit in their lives.	Apple slices

Before the Study

Set out Bibles, chairs, a blindfold for each preteen, three children's puzzles, paper, pens, pencils, balloons, and apple slices. Also make enough photocopies of the "Let the Spirit Speak" handout (p. 32) and "The Spirit's Fruit" handout (p. 33) for each preteen to have one of each.

The Study

Warm-Up Option 1

How Much Guidance Do You Need? *(up to 10 minutes)*

Have preteens form three groups, and give each group a 50- to 75-piece children's puzzle. Tell one group that it must put the puzzle together without looking at the picture on the box. Tell another group that it may look at the picture as it puts the puzzle together. And tell the third group that it must put the puzzle together upside down (with the picture facing down) without looking at the picture.

On "go," have groups work on putting the puzzles together. After the puzzles are complete, or five minutes have passed, **ask:**

• **Which group had the easiest time completing its puzzle?**

• **What made it easier to complete your puzzle?**

Say: Some of you were given guidance to complete your puzzle. In life, we need guidance in much more important ways. We've been looking at God in three persons. The Holy Spirit is the third person of God. The Holy Spirit works in our lives in many ways. Today we're going to look at how ▶the Holy Spirit teaches and guides us.

◀ *The Point*

Warm-Up Option 2

Looking for Guidance *(up to 10 minutes)*

This activity works best in a room with a carpeted floor. Give each preteen an uninflated balloon. Have kids form three teams for balloon races. Determine a starting and finish line about fifteen feet apart. Then give the following instructions to the three teams:

Members of Team One may not blow up their balloons. They must kick the uninflated balloons to the finish line.

Members of Team Two must get their balloons to the finish line by blowing up the balloons and letting the air out to propel them through the air.

Members of Team Three must blow up their balloons before starting the race, tie them off and, when the race begins, bat them in the air with their hands to the finish line.

Have kids on each team take turns running the race. The third team should easily win the race. After the race, have kids discuss the following questions. **Ask:**

• **If you were on Team One or Two, what was it like trying to run this race?**

• **Why was the race easiest for Team Three (the one with the inflated balloons)?**

Say: In our game, the team with the inflated balloons was able to easily guide its balloons across the finish line. In life, we need guidance in much more important ways. We've been looking at God in three persons. The Holy Spirit is the third person of God. The Holy Spirit works in our lives in many ways. Today we're going to look at how ▶the Holy Spirit teaches and guides us.

◀ *The Point*

Bible Connection

Finding Our Way in the Dark (up to 20 minutes)

Designate starting and ending points for an obstacle course in the room. The ending point should be exiting through a doorway if possible. Show kids where the starting and ending points are.

Form two groups. Have each preteen put on a blindfold. Then arrange chairs and other furniture to create obstacles for the course. Put plenty of chairs between the starting and ending points so that kids will have to walk around lots of objects as if in a life-size maze. Go to the first group, and turn some of the kids in place to disorient them.

Then **say: Your job is to carefully get from this starting point to the ending point. I'll time you and see how long it takes for everyone in the group to reach that point. You may hold on to each other's shoulders or stand in a line, but you must all complete the course before I'll stop timing. You may not talk to each other or move furniture around. If you run into something, go a different way. Ready? Go!**

Time the group, and watch to make sure no one gets hurt running into furniture. After the members of the first group have made it to the ending point, have them wait, with blindfolds still on, until the other group has participated.

On "go," have the second group head toward the ending point, but give this group guidance by calling out directions. Time this group, too.

After both groups have gone through the course, have kids take off their blindfolds and form a circle. Let kids know how long it took for each group to complete the course. **Ask:**

• **How did you feel trying to get through this course?**

• **How is that like the way you feel as you work your way through the obstacles of life?**

• **Which group had the best chance of finishing the course?**

Say: Both groups worked toward the goal of finding the ending point, but one had additional guidance from me. The Holy Spirit can give us direction, just as I gave the second group direction. When Jesus promised the Holy Spirit to the disciples, he explained some of what the Holy Spirit would do.

Ask a volunteer to read John 14:26 aloud.

FYI

Whenever groups discuss a list of questions, write the questions on newsprint, and tape the newsprint to the wall so that groups can discuss the questions at their own pace.

Ask:

• **How does Jesus' promise to send the Holy Spirit to teach you offer you encouragement?**

Give each preteen a photocopy of the "Let the Spirit Speak" handout (p. 32), a pen, and a Bible. Have kids complete the handouts and then find partners to discuss them. After kids have shared, **ask:**

• **How does the Holy Spirit influence our directions in life?**

• **In our obstacle course, you had blindfolds on. What blindfolds can the Holy Spirit remove from our eyes?**

Say: As we grow as Christians, the Spirit of God grows in us. Let's look at ways this occurs.

A Personal Holy Spirit *(up to 15 minutes)*

Give each preteen a Bible, sheet of paper, and a pen. Have kids locate Romans 8:9-16 in their Bibles. **Say: Because the Holy Spirit working in our lives is a personal one, I want you personalize the verses from Romans 8:9-16 on your paper. Rewrite the verses in your own words. Don't worry about covering everything in the Bible passage, just focus on the parts that mean the most to you. Before we begin, let's ask the Holy Spirit to give you an understanding of the Bible passage.**

Pray a prayer similar to this one: **Holy Spirit, teach us and give us understanding of these verses. Amen.**

Give kids a few minutes to write their verses. After a few minutes, allow volunteers to read what they wrote and give an explanation of why they wrote it.

Ask:

• **How do you think the Holy Spirit helped you write your verses?**

• **What other Bible verses do you need the Holy Spirit to help you understand?**

Say: We've been exploring ways ➤the Holy Spirit teaches and guides us. Let's look at one more way we can have the Holy Spirit in our lives.

◄ *The Point*

Life Application

Fruit in My Life (up to 10 minutes)

Give each preteen a photocopy of the "Spirit's Fruit" handout and a pencil. **Say: The Holy Spirit gives us qualities that help us live lives that please God. On your handout, you'll see that these qualities are called the fruit of the Spirit.**

Have kids follow the directions on the handout, and give them several minutes to complete the handouts.

Ask:

• **What things did the Holy Spirit teach you as you filled out each of the fruits on the handout?**

• **How can the Spirit help you grow in the areas you need to?**

• **How do you think you can ask the Holy Spirit to help you grow?**

The Point ➤ **Say:** ➤**The Holy Spirit teaches and guides us. And one way we can ask God to send his Holy Spirit to live in us is to pray. Let's do that now.**

Wrap-Up Option 1

Anointing Power (up to 5 minutes)

Say: Many symbols for the Holy Spirit are used in the Bible. One symbol is oil. Oil was used to anoint priests, prophets, and kings in the Old Testament to symbolize the presence of the Holy Spirit in their lives. Oil in the New Testament also represented the healing power of the Spirit.

Have kids form a circle and hold hands.

Say: I'll begin a prayer aloud, then have you repeat the prayer after me. As you repeat this prayer, imagine what it might've felt like being anointed by the elders as was the custom in Bible times.

Read the following prayer aloud, pausing for kids to repeat after you. **Holy Spirit, teach my mind God's Word.** (Pause.) **Holy Spirit, open my ears to truth.** (Pause.) **Holy Spirit, anoint my words with sounds that are pleasing to you.** (Pause.) **Holy Spirit, empower my hands to serve you.** (Pause.) **Holy Spirit, guide my footsteps in the way of the Lord.** (Pause.) **Amen.**

Wrap-Up Option 2

A Fruitful Prayer (up to 5 minutes)

Give each preteen an apple slice. Have kids form a circle. **Say: Since we've**

FYI

Both Wrap-Up activities involve prayer. The first option introduces another concept about the Holy Spirit. The second continues the theme of the fruit of the Spirit. If you are running short of time, you could simply pray the prayer in Option 1, leaving out the section about oil.

just learned about the fruit of the Spirit, let's ask God to grow this fruit in our lives. I'll start a prayer and then pause for each of us to silently complete the prayer.

Holy Spirit, grow in me the fruit of...

After a minute, say "amen" and let kids eat their apple slices.

Extra-Time Tips

Use these extra ideas to add some creative fun to your studies. They are low-prep or no-prep ideas that work in no time!

More Questions—Have kids form a circle and call out questions they have about the Holy Spirit. Encourage other kids to use their Bibles as they answer the questions. Tell preteens that we don't fully understand all the questions we may have about God or the Holy Spirit but that God is pleased as we continue to seek answers.

Invisible, But Real—Have kids form groups to pantomime how the Holy Spirit works through people. Help kids see how, though we can't see the Holy Spirit, we know the Holy Spirit is real.

Let the Spirit Speak

Read John 16:6-16 and then answer the following questions. When you've completed the handout, find a partner and talk together about your completed handouts. If you don't feel comfortable talking about every issue with your partner, choose one or two you do feel comfortable discussing.

The Holy Spirit...

...convicts us of sin. What is an area of sin in your life that the Spirit is leading you to confess and be forgiven?

_____

_____

_____

...directs us toward righteousness. What is something in your life the Spirit is encouraging you to do to serve Jesus better?

_____

_____

_____

...helps us overcome temptation. What temptations are you dealing with that you need strength from the Holy Spirit to resist?

_____

_____

_____

...teaches truth. What new truth that you've learned about the Holy Spirit excites you most?

_____

_____

_____

...gives glory to Jesus Christ. What is one way you desire to glorify and give praise to Jesus Christ?

_____

_____

_____

The Spirit's Fruit

The tree below represents the fruit of the Spirit given to us. Look up Galatians 5:22-23a. Label each fruit with the name of a fruit of the Spirit described in this passage. Then shade each fruit to the degree you're living that attribute or characteristic. For example, if you're kind to most people, you might shade half of that fruit. If patience is difficult for you, you might only shade a small portion of that fruit.

Knowing Jesus

The Point: ➤ Jesus wants to be our best friend.

Preteens are at a stage in their development where having close friendships is important. But friendships for young adolescents can be difficult. One week Sara and Karly are best friends, and the next week they may not speak to each other. Preteens need to know that, even though their friendships go through tough times, they can always count on Jesus being their very best friend. Best friends stay together even when the bottom of life is collapsing. This was Jesus' promise: "I will be with you always" to laugh, play, work, cry, eat, sigh, and celebrate, and to talk to every day.

Scripture Source

John 13:1-17

Jesus demonstrates selfless humility as he washes the feet of his disciples. He gives a powerful example of how his friendship and love for them could be shown.

John 15:12-15

Jesus describes the true meaning of love for a friend. Jesus displays the most radical friendship by laying down his life for "his friends," literally "the ones he loves." Jesus magnified the normal, everyday use of the word *friend* by his sacrificial act.

Romans 5:6-11

Paul describes how Jesus died for everyone. Jesus died for us at the right time, as the ultimate sacrifice and demonstration of his love for humankind. Being justified by Jesus' blood means we are reconciled to God.

The Study at a Glance

Section	Minutes	What Students Will Do	Supplies
Warm-Up Option 1	up to 10	**Friendship Challenge**—Compete in a challenge to gain new friends.	
Warm-Up Option 2	up to 10	**Friendship Symbols**—Create symbols representing friendship.	Chenille wires
Bible Connection	up to 15	**Friendship Auction**—Try to "win" friendship traits and then explore John 13:1-17.	Bibles, "Friendship Traits" handouts (p. 42), pens
	up to 15	**Friendship Cards From Jesus**—Give each other cards of encouragement as if written by Jesus, then discuss John 15:12-15.	Bibles, "Friendship Bible Passages" handouts (p. 43), paper, markers
Life Application	up to 10	**Making Jesus *Your* Friend**—Write Romans 5:6-11 in their own words before committing to follow Jesus.	Bibles, index cards, pens
Wrap-Up Option 1	up to 5	**Friend to Friend**—Participate in a group prayer and thank Jesus for being their best friend.	
Wrap-Up Option 2	up to 5	**Friends Forever**—Brainstorm things that make friendships last.	Bible

Before the Study

Set out Bibles, chenille wires, paper, markers, index cards, and pens. Also, make enough photocopies of the "Friendship Traits" handout (p. 42) and "Friendship Bible Passages" handout (p. 43) for each preteen to have one of each.

The Study

Warm-Up Option 1

Friendship Challenge *(up to 10 minutes)*

Ask for two or three volunteers. If your group is larger than twelve, ask for one volunteer for every four people in your class. **Say: We're going to see which of these volunteers can gain the most friends within four minutes. The rules of this activity are simple: The volunteers may use any means necessary to gain friendships with the other class members. For example, they may attempt to bribe people, give them compliments, or simply be nice to them. After time is up, I'll ask class members to choose which one volunteer they'll be friends with. For this activity, ignore how you feel about the people in real life, and** base your decision solely on the next four minutes. Ready? Go.

After four minutes, call time. Have class members go and stand next to the volunteers they choose to be friends with. This activity may bring out feelings of unpopularity in volunteers. Remind kids that this is just an exercise, but be prepared to talk to kids about their feelings if they seem upset by the outcome of the game.

Ask:

• **How did you feel as the volunteers tried to make you their friends?**

• **How is that like or unlike the way people become friends in real life?**

• **What methods did volunteers use to develop friendships?**

• **What are the best ways to develop friendships?**

Say: In this activity, you had to try to convince people to be your friends. But there is one friendship in which you don't need to do any of these things. Today we'll explore how ➤Jesus wants to be our best friend…for life!   ◀ *The Point*

Warm-Up Option 2

Friendship Symbols *(up to 10 minutes)*

Have preteens form groups of no more than five. Give groups each a supply of chenille wires. **Say:** In the next three minutes, talk with your group members about what you could make with your chenille wires. You can use the chenille wires with any other item in the room except another group's chenille wires.

The object you create must somehow represent something about friendship. For example, you could create something as simple as a heart shape to represent the love friends have for each other. Make sure each person in your group helps with this project.

Allow a few minutes for groups to create their items. Then have each group describe what it created.

Ask:

• **How did you feel about working together in your group to create these friendship symbols?**

• **How is this like the way people feel when they're developing friendships?**

Say: In this activity, you had to work with different people. Some of the people in your group you may be friends with, while others you may not be. It takes time to build friendships with people. But there is one friendship that you can have right now. Today we'll explore how ➤Jesus wants to be our best friend...for life!

Bible Connection

Friendship Auction *(up to 15 minutes)*

Give each preteen a photocopy of the "Friendship Traits" handout (p. 42) and a pen. **Say:** In a minute, you'll have the opportunity to "win" some of the traits described on this handout.

The object of this activity is to win as many of these traits as possible. The way you do this is by demonstrating the trait you want to as many people as possible during the time available. Once you've demonstrated that trait, the person you're demonstrating it to must sign his or her name next to the item on your handout. But the trick is that you may not say which trait you're demonstrating. You may speak, but not specifically about the trait you're going after. Remember that integrity is one of these items, so be honest.

When time is up, we'll see who has the most signatures for each item. Choose the traits you think are most important.

Give kids time to read the handout. Then, on "go," have preteens go around demonstrating friendship traits to each other.

After about five minutes, call time and have kids sit in a circle. Read each item on the handout, and find out who has the most signatures for that item. Then **ask:**

• **How did you feel as you demonstrated friendship traits to each other?**

• **How did you feel as you were shown friendship traits by others?**

• **How is this like the way you feel when someone reaches out to you in friendship?**

• **Did any of the traits seem unusual to you? Explain.**

Say: Jesus spent over three years with his disciples. They were his special friends. Let's explore a time Jesus did an unusual thing for his friends.

Ask for several volunteers to each read several verses of John 13:1-17 aloud. **Ask:**

• **If you had been one of the disciples, how do you think you would have reacted to Jesus washing your feet?**

• **What quality of friendship would Jesus' actions show?**

Say: Foot-washing was a dirty job in Bible times. People walked on dirt

FYI

Whenever groups discuss a list of questions, write the questions on newsprint, and tape the newsprint to the wall so that groups can discuss the questions at their own pace.

roads wearing only sandals, and their feet got *very* dirty. Normally, servants would wash people's feet, but Jesus chose to do this task for his friends.

Ask:

• How has a friend served you or have you served a friend?

Say: There are many ways we can serve our friends or be served by them. But our friends can never serve us as completely as Jesus can. ➤Jesus wants to be our best friend. Let's see some ways he can be this.

◀ *The Point*

Friendship Cards From Jesus *(up to 15 minutes)*

Say: Best friends say encouraging and supporting words when they're working together toward a goal. They celebrate the joys of their triumphs and hold on to each other when things are falling to pieces. According to this definition, Jesus must then be our best friend.

Give each preteen two or three sheets of paper, a marker, a Bible, and a photocopy of the "Friendship Bible Passages" handout (p. 43). **Say:** Choose at least three passages from the "Friendship Bible Passages" handout, and read them. Then use your paper and marker to design your own "Friendship Card From Jesus" based on the meaning of that passage.

For example, if you read John 10:14-15, you might design a card with sheep on the front and a message on the inside describing how much Jesus cares for you. Word the message as if Jesus were writing this card to you. Here's an example from the John 10:14-15 passage:

I would lay down my life for you.

In fact, I did!

You are that important to me. I love you!

Your Best Friend,

Jesus

Allow enough time for preteens to read the Bible passages and create three friendship cards. Then have kids form trios and talk about the messages in their cards and why it's important to see Jesus as a friend. Allow volunteers to share what they wrote on their cards. Then **say:** There is one thing Jesus did that clearly makes him our very best friend.

Have a volunteer read aloud John 15:12-15.

Ask:

- How does this passage make you feel?
- Would it be easy to lay down your life for a friend? Why or why not?
- How do you feel about Jesus' friendship?

Say: It is possible that a friend might die for you. But only Jesus can die for you for the best reason possible. Let's see what that is.

Life Application

Making Jesus *Your* Friend (up to 10 minutes)

Give preteens Bibles, index cards, and pens. Ask a volunteer to read Romans 5:6-8. **Say: Only Jesus could die to save us from our sins.** ➤**Jesus wants to be our best friend. The only thing we need to do is believe in him. Some of you may be thinking about becoming a friend of Jesus, while some of you are already believers in Jesus.**

Ask kids to write Romans 5:6-8 in their own words on one side of their index cards. Then ask a volunteer to read Romans 5:9-11. **Say: This is the promise of having a relationship with Jesus.**

Ask kids to write Romans 5:9-11 in their own words on the other side of their index cards. Then **say: Choosing Jesus to be your best friend is the most important decision you'll make in your life. I'm going to give you a few minutes to reflect on your relationship with Jesus. You may read the verses on your index cards, pray to God, or just think about what you've discovered today.**

Allow a few minutes for kids to reflect before moving to the Wrap-Up activity of your choice.

Wrap-Up Option 1

Friend to Friend (up to 5 minutes)

Have preteens form a circle. **Say: Our friends can encourage us and help us grow as Christians. Let's thank God for our friendships. I'll let you pray silently for about a minute, then we'll close by you repeating the words I'll say. Let's pray now.**

Allow a minute for silent prayer. Then have kids repeat after you in unison: **Thank you for giving us friends we can talk to, (pause) be encouraged by,**

The Point ➤

FYI

Be available to talk to any preteens who want to have a personal relationship with Jesus or to talk to kids about their relationship with Jesus. Talk to your pastor if you need assistance in guiding a preteen's relationship with Jesus.

(pause) **help when we can,** (pause) **and grow close to. And thank you for Jesus' friendship being the best.** (Pause.) **Amen.**

Wrap-Up Option 2

Friends Forever *(up to 5 minutes)*

Have kids form pairs and each say at least one thing they believe makes friendships last, such as honesty, patience, and love. Then have kids pray that their partners exhibit those qualities in their own friendships. Encourage kids to ask Jesus to show them how to be the friend Jesus would want them to be.

Close by reading John 15:12-15 to remind kids about Jesus' ultimate act of friendship.

Extra-Time Tips

Use these extra ideas to add some creative fun to your studies. They are low-prep or no-prep ideas that work in no time!

Foot-washing—Have a couple of pans of warm water and towels available for the students to wash each other's feet. After the experience, have kids discuss how they felt serving each other.

Ask:

- **What role does serving play in friendships?**

- **How easy is it to serve your friends?**

Have kids read and discuss John 13:1-17.

Ask:

- **What can we learn from Jesus' serving attitude?**

Best Friends—Have each preteen write a short poem about his or her best friend or what it takes to be a best friend. Encourage kids to include characteristics Jesus displays. Then have preteens read their poems aloud. Afterward, have kids discuss what it means to be a best friend.

FYI

Encourage preteens to save their "Friendship Bible Passages" handouts and commit to reading the passages over the next few weeks. The handout has instructions for kids to follow. You might want to encourage kids during this time with a brief phone or e-mail message.

Friendship Traits

- Support
  _____

- Kindness
  _____

- Honesty
  _____

- Love
  _____

- A servant attitude
  _____

- Forgiveness
  _____

- Concern
  _____

- Encouragement
  _____

- Sense of humor
  _____

Friendship Bible Passages

Choose three of the following passages to read and use to create "Friendship Cards From Jesus."

John 3:16-17	John 11:35-36
John 4:13-14	John 13:1-9
John 5:6-9	John 14:1-6
John 5:24	John 14:12-14
John 6:16-20	John 14:15-21
John 6:35	John 14:26-27
John 8:6-11	John 15:5
John 8:12	John 15:9-17
John 8:31-36	John 16:20-22
John 9:1-7	John 16:23-24
John 10:9-10	John 17:20-23
John 10:14-15	John 20:19-23
John 10:27-30	John 20:29
John 11:25-27	John 21:15-17

Save this handout, and use it as a starting place for discovering more about your friend Jesus. Read one passage each day for the next few weeks. Then meet with a friend to discuss the passages.

This study has looked at helping preteens understand God in three persons: God, Jesus Christ, and the Holy Spirit. As preteens make independent decisions about the faith many of them have been taught through their childhood years, this activity will help them make personal decisions.

Who Is Jesus? Survey

Have preteens decorate a box with an opening cut in the top of it. Place the box at the back of your church one Sunday. Arrange with the pastor to allow the preteens to distribute index cards to the congregation gathered. Have a preteen explain to the congregation that they are learning about God, Jesus, and the Holy Spirit. Have the preteen ask the congregation to answer the question "Who is Jesus to you?" and explain that they can drop the cards in the box at the back of the church on their way out.

Plan a meeting where kids can read the cards and discuss them. You might want to invite your pastor to the meeting to help answer questions about the responses on the cards. Some of the responses on the cards may have ideas that conflict with your church's teaching. Use the discussion as an opportunity to explore what the Bible does and does not say about Jesus, as appropriate.

Group Publishing, Inc.
Attention: Product Development
P.O. Box 481
Loveland, CO 80539
Fax: (970) 679-4370

Evaluation for
Faith 4 Life: Preteen Bible Study Series
God in My Life

Please help Group Publishing, Inc., continue to provide innovative and useful resources for ministry. Please take a moment to fill out this evaluation and mail or fax it to us. Thanks!

● ● ●

1. As a whole, this book has been (circle one)

not very helpful   very helpful

1   2   3   4   5   6   7   8   9   10

2. The best things about this book:

3. Ways this book could be improved:

4. Things I will change because of this book:

5. Other books I'd like to see Group publish in the future:

6. Would you be interested in field-testing future Group products and giving us your feedback? If so, please fill in the information below:

Name _____

Church Name _____

Denomination _____ Church Size _____

Church Address _____

City _____ State _____ ZIP _____

Church Phone _____

E-mail _____

Look for the Whole Family of Faith 4 Life Bible Studies!

Preteen Books
Being Responsible
Getting Along With Others

God in My Life
Going Through Tough Times

Junior High Books
Becoming a Christian
Finding Your Identity

God's Purpose for Me
Understanding the Bible

Senior High Books
Family Matters
Is There Life After High School?

Prayer
Sharing Your Faith

Coming Soon...

For Preteens
Building Friendships
Handling Conflict
How to Make Great Choices
Peer Pressure

Succeeding in School
The Bible and Me
What's a Christian?
Why God Made Me

For Junior High
Choosing Wisely
Fighting Temptation
Friends
How to Pray

My Family Life
My Life as a Christian
Sharing Jesus
Who Is God?

For Senior High
Applying God's Word
Believing in Jesus
Christian Character
Following Jesus

Sexuality
Worshipping 24/7
Your Christian ID
Your Relationships

Visit your local Christian bookstore or contact Group Publishing, Inc., at 800-447-1070. www.grouppublishing.com

More Preteen Ministry Resources!

The Preteen Worker's Encyclopedia of Bible-Teaching Ideas

Make the New Testament come alive to your preteens and help them discover Bible truths in a big way! In this comprehensive collection, you get nearly 200 creative ideas and activities including: object lessons, skits, games, devotions, service projects, creative prayers, affirmations, creative readings, retreats, parties, trips and travel, and music ideas.

Flexible for any group setting, you'll easily find the perfect idea with helpful Scripture and theme indexes.

ISBN 0-7644-2425-4

Dynamic Preteen Ministry

Gordon West & Becki West

Maximize ministry to preteens as they make the difficult transition from childhood to adolescence. Both children's and youth workers will better understand the minds and emotions of 10- to 14-year-olds, "bridge the gap" between children's ministry and youth ministry.

ISBN 0-7644-2084-4

No-Miss Lessons for Preteen Kids

Here are 22 faith-building lessons that keep 5th- and 6th-graders coming back! Children's workers get active-learning lessons dealing with faith…self-esteem…relationships…choices…and age-appropriate service projects that any preteen class can do!

ISBN 0-7644-2015-1

No-Miss Lessons for Preteen Kids 2

Enjoy ministering to your preteens like never before! This flexible resource features 20 action-packed, easy-to-teach lessons that talk about the stuff of life in the preteen world. Stuff like the Internet and media, how to get along with family and friends, faith foundations based on God and Jesus, and many others! These lessons and the 13 bonus, "can't-miss" service project ideas will challenge kids, grow their faith, and give them practical ideas for living out their deepening faith in meaningful ways!

ISBN 0-7644-2290-1

More Preteen Ministry Resources!

(continued)

The Ultimate Book of Preteen Games

They're not children. Not teenagers. What do you do with preteens? Have a blast! Start with these 100 games they'll love! In the process, you'll break down cliques, build relationships, explore relevant Bible truths, give thought-provoking challenges, and have high-energy fun!

ISBN 0-7644-2291-X

Emotion Explosion!: 40 Devotions for Preteen Ministry

Carol Mader

Show preteens that God understands their confusing emotions and cares about how they feel. With these 40 fun devotions based on the Psalms, preteens will explore the highs and lows of the life of David, and learn to take their feelings of doubt and sorrow, hope and joy to God. Group games and activities make this the perfect devotional for preteens.

Reproducibles included!

ISBN 0-7644-2221-9

Order today from your local Christian bookstore, online at www.faithweaver.com or write:
Group Publishing, P.O. Box 485, Loveland, CO 80539-0485.